The Key Facts™ on

The European

Union

Essential Information on the European

Union

By Patrick W. Nee

The Internationalist®

www.internationalist.com

The Internationalist®

International Business, Investment, and Travel

Published by:

The Internationalist Publishing Company

96 Walter Street/ Suite 200

Boston, MA 02131, USA

Tel: 617-354-7722

www.internationalist.com

PN@internationalist.com

Table Of Contents

Chapter 1: Introduction & Background

Chapter 2: Geography

Chapter 3: People and Society

Chapter 4: Government

Chapter 5: Economy

Chapter 6: Energy

Chapter 7: Communications

Chapter 8: Transportation

Chapter 9: Military

Chapter 10: Transnational Issues

Chapter 1: Introduction & Background

Preliminary statement:

The evolution of what is today the European Union (EU) from a regional economic agreement among six neighboring states in 1951 to today's hybrid intergovernmental and supranational organization of 27 countries across the European continent stands as an unprecedented phenomenon in the annals of history. Dynastic unions for territorial consolidation were long the norm in Europe; on a few occasions even country-level unions were arranged - the Polish-Lithuanian Commonwealth and the Austro-Hungarian Empire were examples. But for such a large number of nation-states to cede some of their sovereignty to an overarching entity is unique.

Although the EU is not a federation in the strict sense, it is far more than a free-trade association such as ASEAN, NAFTA, or Mercosur, and it has certain attributes associated with independent nations: its own flag, currency (for some members), and law-making abilities, as well as diplomatic representation and a common foreign and security policy in its dealings with external partners. Thus, inclusion of basic intelligence on the EU has been deemed appropriate as a new, separate entity in The World

Factbook. However, because of the EU's special status, this description is placed after the regular country entries.

Background:

Following the two devastating World Wars in the first half of the 20th century, a number of European leaders in the late 1940s became convinced that the only way to establish a lasting peace was to reconcile the two chief belligerent nations - France and Germany - both economically and politically. In 1950, the French Foreign Minister Robert SCHUMAN proposed an eventual union of all Europe, the first step of which would be the integration of the coal and steel industries of Western Europe. The following year the European Coal and Steel Community (ECSC) was set up when six members, Belgium, France, West Germany, Italy, Luxembourg, and the Netherlands, signed the Treaty of Paris.

The ECSC was so successful that within a few years the decision was made to integrate other elements of the countries' economies. In 1957, envisioning an "ever closer union," the Treaties of Rome created the European Economic Community (EEC) and the European Atomic Energy Community (Euratom), and the six member states undertook to eliminate trade barriers among themselves by forming a common market. In 1967, the institutions of all three communities were formally merged into the European Community (EC), creating a single Commission, a single Council of Ministers, and the body known today as the European Parliament. Members of the European Parliament were initially selected by national parliaments, but in 1979 the first direct elections were undertaken and they have been held every five years since.

In 1973, the first enlargement of the EC took place with the addition of Denmark, Ireland, and the United Kingdom. The 1980s saw further membership expansion with Greece joining in 1981 and Spain and Portugal in 1986. The 1992 Treaty of Maastricht laid the basis for further forms of cooperation in foreign and defense policy, in judicial and internal affairs, and in the creation of an economic and monetary union - including a common currency. This further integration created the European Union (EU), at the time standing alongside the European Community. In 1995, Austria, Finland, and Sweden joined the EU/EC, raising the membership total to 15.

A new currency, the euro, was launched in world money markets on 1 January 1999; it became the unit of exchange for all EU member states except the United Kingdom, Sweden, and Denmark. In 2002, citizens of those 12 countries began using euro banknotes and coins. Ten new countries joined the EU in 2004 - Cyprus, the Czech Republic, Estonia, Hungary, Latvia, Lithuania, Malta, Poland, Slovakia, and Slovenia - and in 2007 Bulgaria and

Romania joined, bringing the membership to 27, where it stands today.

In an effort to ensure that the EU could function efficiently with an expanded membership, the Treaty of Nice (signed in 2000) set forth rules aimed at streamlining the size and procedures of EU institutions. An effort to establish a "Constitution for Europe," growing out of a Convention held in 2002-2003, foundered when it was rejected in referenda in France and the Netherlands in 2005. A subsequent effort in 2007 incorporated many of the features of the rejected Constitution while also making a number of substantive and symbolic changes. The new treaty, initially known as the Reform Treaty but subsequently referred to as the Treaty of Lisbon, sought to amend existing treaties rather than replace them. The treaty was approved at the EU intergovernmental conference of the 27 member states held in Lisbon in December 2007, after which the process of national ratifications began. In October 2009, an Irish referendum approved the Lisbon Treaty (overturning a previous rejection) and cleared the way for an ultimate unanimous endorsement. Poland and the Czech Republic signed on soon after. The Lisbon Treaty, again invoking the idea of an "ever closer union," came into force on 1 December 2009 and the European Union officially replaced and succeeded the European Community.

Chapter 2: Geography

Location:

Europe between the North Atlantic Ocean in the west and
Russia, Belarus, and Ukraine to the east

Map references:

Europe

Area:

total: 4,324,782 sq km

Area - comparative:

Less than one-half the size of the US

Land boundaries:

Total: 12,440.8 km

Border countries: Albania 282 km, Andorra 120.3 km,
Belarus 1,050 km, Croatia 999 km, Holy See 3.2 km,
Liechtenstein 34.9 km, Macedonia 394 km, Moldova 450
km, Monaco 4.4 km, Norway 2,348 km, Russia 2,257 km,
San Marino 39 km, Serbia 945 km, Switzerland 1,811 km,
Turkey 446 km, Ukraine 1,257 km

Note: data for European Continent only

Coastline:

65,992.9 km

Maritime claims:

NA

Climate:

Cold temperate; potentially subarctic in the north to temperate; mild wet winters; hot dry summers in the south

Terrain:

Fairly flat along the Baltic and Atlantic coast; mountainous in the central and southern areas

Elevation extremes:

Lowest point: Lammefjord, Denmark -7 m; Zuidplaspolder, Netherlands -7 m

Highest point: Mont Blanc 4,807 m; note - situated on the border between France and Italy

Natural resources:

Iron ore, natural gas, petroleum, coal, copper, lead, zinc, bauxite, uranium, potash, salt, hydropower, arable land, timber, fish

Irrigated land:

182,913 sq km (2003 est.)

Natural hazards:

Flooding along coasts; avalanches in mountainous area; earthquakes in the south; volcanic eruptions in Italy; periodic droughts in Spain; ice floes in the Baltic

Environment - international agreements:

Party to: Air Pollution, Air Pollution-Nitrogen Oxides, Air Pollution-Persistent Organic Pollutants, Air Pollution-Sulphur 94, Antarctic-Marine Living Resources, Biodiversity, Climate Change, Climate Change-Kyoto Protocol, Desertification, Hazardous Wastes, Law of the

Sea, Ozone Layer Protection, Tropical Timber 83,
Tropical Timber 94
<u>Signed but not ratified</u>: Air Pollution-Volatile Organic
Compounds

Chapter 3: People and Society

Languages:

Bulgarian, Czech, Danish, Dutch, English, Estonian, Finnish, French, Gaelic, German, Greek, Hungarian, Italian, Latvian, Lithuanian, Maltese, Polish, Portuguese, Romanian, Slovak, Slovene, Spanish, Swedish

Note: only official languages are listed; German, the major language of Germany, Austria, and Switzerland, is the most widely spoken mother tongue - about 18% of the EU population; English is the most widely spoken foreign language - about 38% of the EU population is conversant with it (2013)

Religions:

Roman Catholic, Protestant, Orthodox, Muslim, Jewish

Population:

503,824,373 (July 2012 est.)

Age structure:

0-14 years: 15.45% (male 39,926,647/female 37,906,680)

15-24 years: 11.57% (male 29,794,390/female 28,495,558)

25-54 years: 42.49% (male 107,822,096/female 106,244,651)

55-64 years: 12.6% (male 30,778,919/female 32,682,293)

65 years and over: 17.9% (male 38,139,934/female 52,033,205) (2012 est.)

Population growth rate:

0.212% (2012 est.)

Birth rate:

10.27 births/1,000 population (2012 est.)

Death rate:

10.05 deaths/1,000 population (July 2012 est.)

Net migration rate:

1.90 migrant(s)/1,000 population (2012 est.)

Sex ratio:

At birth: 1.06 male(s)/female

Under 15 years: 1.05 male(s)/female

15-64 years: 1 male(s)/female

65 years and over: 0.73 male(s)/female

Total population: 0.96 male(s)/female (2012 est.)

Infant mortality rate:

Total: 4.49 deaths/1,000 live births

Country comparison to the world: 190

Male: 4.96 deaths/1,000 live births

Female: 3.99 deaths/1,000 live births (2012 est.)

Life expectancy at birth:

Total population: 79.76 years

Country comparison to the world: 36

Male: 76.91 years

Female: 82.76 years (2012 est.)

Total fertility rate:

1.58 children born/woman (2012 est.)

Chapter 4: Government

Union name:

    <u>Conventional long form</u>: European Union

    <u>Abbreviation</u>: EU

Political structure:

    A hybrid and unique intergovernmental and supranational organization

Capital:

    <u>Name</u>: Brussels (Belgium), Strasbourg (France), Luxembourg

    <u>Geographic coordinates</u>: (Brussels) 50 50 N, 4 20 E

    <u>Time difference</u>: UTC+1 (6 hours ahead of Washington, DC during Standard Time)

    daylight saving time: +1hr, begins last Sunday in March; ends last Sunday in October

    <u>Note</u>: the European Council and the Council of the European Union meet in Brussels, Belgium; the European Parliament meets in Brussels and Strasbourg, France, and has administrative offices in Luxembourg; the Court of Justice of the European Union meets in Luxembourg

Member states:

    <u>27 countries</u>: Austria, Belgium, Bulgaria, Cyprus, Czech Republic, Denmark, Estonia, Finland, France, Germany, Greece, Hungary, Ireland, Italy, Latvia, Lithuania, Luxembourg, Malta, Netherlands, Poland, Portugal,

Romania, Slovakia, Slovenia, Spain, Sweden, UK; note - candidate countries: Croatia, Iceland, Macedonia, Montenegro, Serbia, Turkey

Independence:

7 February 1992 (Maastricht Treaty signed establishing the European Union); 1 November 1993 (Maastricht Treaty entered into force)

Note: the Treaties of Rome, signed on 25 March 1957 and subsequently entered into force on 1 January 1958, created the European Economic Community and the European Atomic Energy Community; a series of subsequent treaties have been adopted to increase efficiency and transparency, to prepare for new member states, and to introduce new areas of cooperation - such as single currency; the Treaty of Lisbon, signed on 13 December 2007 and entered into force on 1 December 2009 is the most recent of these treaties and is intended to make the EU more democratic, more efficient, and better able to address global problems with one voice

National holiday:

Europe Day 9 May (1950); note - the day in 1950 that Robert SCHUMAN proposed the creation of what became the European Coal and Steel Community, the progenitor of today's European Union, with the aim of achieving a united Europe

Constitution:

None

Note: the EU legal order, although based on a series of treaties, has often been described as "constitutional" in nature; the Treaty on European Union (TEU), as modified by the Lisbon Treaty, states in Article 1 that "the HIGH CONTRACTING PARTIES establish among themselves a EUROPEAN UNION ... on which the Member States confer competences to attain objectives they have in common"; Article 1 of the TEU states further that the EU is "founded on the present Treaty and on the Treaty on the Functioning of the European Union (hereinafter referred to as 'the Treaties')," both possessing the same legal value; Article 6 of the TEU provides that a separately adopted Charter of Fundamental Rights of the European Union "shall have the same legal value as the Treaties"

Legal system:

Unique supranational law system in which, according to an interpretive declaration of member-state governments appended to the Treaty of Lisbon, "the Treaties and the law adopted by the Union on the basis of the Treaties have primacy over the law of Member States" under conditions laid down in the case law of the Court of Justice; key principles of EU law include fundamental rights as guaranteed by the Charter of Fundamental Rights and as resulting from constitutional traditions common to the EU's states; EU law is divided into 'primary' and 'secondary' legislation; the treaties (primary legislation) are the basis for all EU action; secondary legislation - which includes regulations, directives and decisions - are derived from the principles and objectives set out in the treaties

Suffrage:

18 years of age; universal; voting for the European Parliament is permitted in each member state

Executive branch:

Under the EU treaties there are three distinct institutions, each of which conducts functions that may be regarded as executive in nature:

The European Council: brings together heads of state and government, along with the president of the European Commission, and meets at least four times a year; its aim is to provide the impetus for the development of the Union and to issue general policy guidelines; leaders of the EU member states appointed former Belgian Prime Minister Herman VAN ROMPUY to be the first full-time president of the European Council in November 2009; he took office on 1 December 2009 for a two-and-one-half-year term, renewable once; EU member state leaders confirmed VAN ROMPUY for a second and final two-and-one-half-year term in March 2012; his core responsibilities include chairing the EU summits and providing policy and organizational continuity

The Council of the European Union: consists of ministers of each EU member state and meets regularly in different configurations depending on the subject matter; it carries out policy-making and coordinating functions (as well as legislative functions); ministers of EU member states chair meetings of the Council of the EU based on a six-month rotating presidency

The European Commission: is headed by a College of Commissioners comprised of 27 members, one from each member country; each commissioner is responsible for one or more policy areas; the Commission's responsibilities include the sole right to initiate EU legislation (except for foreign and defense policy), promoting the general interest of the EU, acting as "guardian of the Treaties," executing the budget and managing programs, ensuring the Union's external representation, and additional duties; its president is Jose Manuel BARROSO (since 2004); the president of the European Commission is designated by member state governments and confirmed by the European Parliament; working from member state recommendations, the Commission president then assembles the "college" of Commission members; the European Parliament confirms the entire Commission for a five-year term; the next confirmation process will likely be held in January 2015

Note: for external representation and foreign policy making, leaders of the EU member states appointed

Catherine ASHTON of the United Kingdom to be the first High Representative of the Union for Foreign Affairs and Security Policy; ASHTON took office on 1 December 2009; her concurrent appointment as Vice President of the European Commission endows her position with the policymaking influence of the Council of the EU and the budgetary influence of the European Commission; the High Representative helps develop and implement the EU's Common Foreign and Security Policy (CFSP) and Common Security and Defense Policy (CSDP), chairs the Foreign Affairs Council, represents and acts for the Union in many international contexts, and oversees the European External Action Service (EEAS), the diplomatic corps of the EU, established on 1 December 2010

Legislative branch:

Two legislative bodies consisting of the Council of the European Union (27 member-state ministers having 345 votes; the number of votes is roughly proportional to member-states' population, and 255 votes plus a majority of member states forms a "qualified majority" to pass a measure) and the European Parliament (754 seats; seats allocated among member states in proportion to population; members elected by direct universal suffrage for a five-year term); note - the European Parliament President is elected by a majority of fellow members of the European Parliament (MEP), and represents the Parliament with the EU and internationally; German MEP Martin SCHULZ from the Group of the Progressive Alliance of Socialists and Democrats (S&D) was elected in January 2012; the Council of the EU is the main decision-making body of the EU, although the European Parliament must also approve almost all EU legislation; the Parliament does not have the right to initiate legislation

Elections: last held on 4-7 June 2009 (next to be held in June 2014)

Election results: percent of vote - EPP 36%, S&D 25%, ALDE 11.4%, Greens/EFA 7.5%, ECR 7.3%, GUE/NGL 4.8%, EFD 4.3%, independents 3.7%; seats by party - EPP 265, S&D 184, ALDE 84, Greens/EFA 55, ECR 54, GUE/NGL 35, EFD 32, nonaffiliated 27, plus 18 "observers"; note - current seats by party as of December 2012 - EPP 270, S&D 189, ALDE 85, Greens/EFA 59, ECR 53, GUE/NGL 34, EFD 34, nonaffiliated 30

Judicial branch:

Court of Justice of the European Union (ensures that the treaties are interpreted and applied uniformly throughout the EU, resolves disputed issues among the EU institutions, issues opinions on questions of EU law referred by member state courts) - 27 judges (one from each member state) appointed for a six-year term; note - the court can sit in chambers, in a "Grand Chamber" of 13 judges, or as the full court; General Court (a court below the Court of Justice) - 27 judges appointed for a six-year term; Civil Service Tribunal - 7 judges appointed for a three-year term

Political parties and leaders:

Confederal Group of the European United Left-Nordic Green Left or GUE/NGL [Gabriele ZIMMER]; Europe of Freedom and Democracy Group or EFD [Nigel FARAGE and Francesco SPERONI]; European Conservatives and Reformists Group or ECR [Martin CALLANAN]; Group of Greens/European Free Alliance or Greens/EFA [Rebecca HARMS and Daniel COHN-BENDIT]; Group of the Alliance of Liberals and Democrats for Europe or ALDE [Guy VERHOFSTADT]; Group of the European People's Party or EPP [Joseph DAUL]; Group of the Progressive Alliance of Socialists and Democrats or S&D [Hannes SWOBODA]

International organization participation:

ARF (dialogue member), ASEAN (dialogue member), Australian Group, BIS, BSEC (observer), CBSS, CERN, EBRD, FAO, FATF, G-8, G-10, G-20, IDA, IEA, IGAD (partners), LAIA (observer), NSG (observer), OAS (observer), OECD, PIF (partner), SAARC (observer), UN (observer), UNRWA (observer), WCO, WTO, ZC (observer)

Diplomatic representation in the US:

<u>Chief of mission</u>: Ambassador Joao VALE DE ALMEIDA

Chancery: 2175 K Street, NW, Washington, DC 20037

Telephone: [1] (202) 862-9500

FAX: [1] (202) 429-1766

Diplomatic representation from the US:

Chief of mission: Ambassador William E. KENNARD

Embassy: 13 Zinnerstraat/Rue Zinner, B-1000 Brussels

Mailing address: same as above

Telephone: [32] (2) 508-2111

FAX: [32] (2) 508-2063

Flag description:

A blue field with 12 five-pointed gold stars arranged in a circle in the center; blue represents the sky of the Western world, the stars are the peoples of Europe in a circle, a symbol of unity; the number of stars is fixed

National symbol(s):

A circle of 12 stars

National anthem:

Name: "Ode to Joy""

Lyrics/music: none/Ludwig VON BEETHOVEN, arranged by Herbert VON KARAJAN

Note: adopted 1972, not in use until 1986; according to the European Union, the song is meant to represent all of Europe rather than just the organization; the song also serves as the anthem for the Council of Europe

Chapter 5: Economy

Economy - overview:

Internally, the EU has abolished trade barriers, adopted a common currency, and is striving toward convergence of living standards. Internationally, the EU aims to bolster Europe's trade position and its political and economic weight. Because of the great differences in per capita income among member states (from $13,000 to $82,000) and in national attitudes toward issues like inflation, debt, and foreign trade, the EU faces difficulties in devising and enforcing common policies. Eleven established EU member states, under the auspices of the European Economic and Monetary Union (EMU), introduced the euro as their common currency on 1 January 1999 (Greece did so two years later). Between 2004 and 2007, 12 states acceded to the EU that are, in general, less advanced economically than the other 15 member states. Of the 12 most recent entrants, only Slovenia (1 January 2007), Cyprus and Malta (1 January 2008), Slovakia (1 January 2009), and Estonia (1 January 2011) have adopted the euro; 10 non-Euro member states, other than the UK and Denmark which have formal opt-outs, are required by EU treaties to adopt the common currency upon meeting fiscal and monetary convergence criteria. Following the 2008-09 global economic crisis, the EU economy saw moderate

GDP growth in 2010 and 2011, but a sovereign debt crisis in the euro zone intensified in 2011 and became the bloc's top economic and political priority. Despite EU/IMF adjustment programs in Greece, Ireland, and Portugal, and consolidation measures in many other EU member states, significant risks to growth remain, including high public debt loads, aging populations, onerous regulations, and fears of debt crisis contagion. In response, euro-zone leaders in 2011 boosted funding levels for the temporary European Financial Stability Facility (EFSF) to almost $600 billion and made loan terms more favorable for crisis-hit countries, and in July 2012 brought the permanent European Stabilization Mechanism (ESM) online, a year earlier than originally planned. In addition, 25 of 27 EU member states (all except the UK and Czech Republic) have indicated their intent to enact a "fiscal compact" treaty to boost long-term budgetary discipline and coordination. In September 2012 the European Central Bank committed to a bond-buying program for troubled euro-zone member states that agree to a formal program of fiscal and structural reforms, aiming to reduce their borrowing costs and restore confidence in the euro zone.

GDP (purchasing power parity):

$15.7 trillion (2012 est.)

Country comparison to the world: 1

$15.67 trillion (2011 est.)

$15.42 trillion (2010 est.)

Note: data are in 2012 US dollars

GDP (official exchange rate):

$16.19 trillion (2012 est.)

GDP - real growth rate:

-0.2% (2012 est.)

Country comparison to the world: 189

1.6% (2011 est.)

2.1% (2010 est.)

GDP - per capita (PPP):

$34,500 (2012 est.)

Country comparison to the world: 39

$34,700 (2011 est.)

$34,300 (2010 est.)

Note: data are in 2012 US dollars

GDP - composition by sector:

Agriculture: 1.8%

Industry: 24.6%

Services: 73.5% (2012 est.)

Labor force:

229 million (2012 est.)

Country comparison to the world: 3

Labor force - by occupation:

Agriculture: 5.3%

Industry: 22.9%

Services: 71.8% (2011 est.)

Unemployment rate:

10.5% (2012 est.)

Country comparison to the world: 114

9.7% (2011)

Household income or consumption by percentage share:

Lowest 10%: 2.9%

Highest 10%: 24% (2011 est.)

Distribution of family income - Gini index:

30.7 (2011 est.)

Country comparison to the world: 113

31.2 (1996 est.)

Investment (gross fixed):

18% of GDP (2012 est.)

Country comparison to the world: 119

Inflation rate (consumer prices):

2.6% (2012 est.)

Country comparison to the world: 59

1.8% (2011 est.)

Central bank discount rate:

1.5% (31 December 2012)

Country comparison to the world: 119

1.75% (31 December 2011)

Note: this is the European Central Bank's rate on the marginal lending facility, which offers overnight credit to banks in the euro area

Commercial bank prime lending rate:

5.9% (31 December 2010 est.)

Country comparison to the world: 123

7.52% (31 December 2009 est.)

Stock of narrow money:

$6.205 trillion (31 December 2011)

Country comparison to the world: 2

$5.542 trillion (31 December 2010)

Note: this is the quantity of money, M1, for the euro area, converted into US dollars at the exchange rate for the date indicated; it excludes the stock of money carried by non-euro-area members of the European Union

Stock of broad money:

$12.27 trillion (31 December 2010 est.)

Country comparison to the world: 4

$11.17 trillion (31 December 2010 est.)

Note: this is the quantity of broad money for the euro area, converted into US dollars at the exchange rate for the date indicated; it excludes the stock of broad money carried by non-euro-area members of the European Union

Stock of domestic credit:

$21.29 trillion (31 December 2011 est.)

Country comparison to the world: 2

$21.81 trillion (31 December 2010 est.)

Note: this figure refers to the euro area only; it excludes credit data for non-euro-area members of the EU

Market value of publicly traded shares:

$7.565 trillion (31 December 2011 est.)

Country comparison to the world: 2

$10.5 trillion (31 December 2010)

$9.823 trillion (31 December 2009 est.)

Agriculture - products:

Wheat, barley, oilseeds, sugar beets, wine, grapes; dairy products, cattle, sheep, pigs, poultry; fish

Industries:

Among the world's largest and most technologically advanced, the EU industrial base includes: ferrous and non-ferrous metal production and processing, metal products, petroleum, coal, cement, chemicals, pharmaceuticals, aerospace, rail transportation equipment, passenger and commercial vehicles, construction equipment, industrial equipment, shipbuilding, electrical power equipment, machine tools and automated manufacturing systems, electronics and telecommunications equipment, fishing, food and beverage processing, furniture, paper, textiles

Industrial production growth rate:

2.8% (2011 est.)

Country comparison to the world: 109

Current account balance:

-$34.49 billion (2011 est.)

Country comparison to the world: 185

-$5.73 billion (2010 est.)

Exports:

$2.17 trillion (2011 est.)

Country comparison to the world: 1

$1.791 trillion (2010 est.)

Note: external exports, excluding intra-EU trade

Exports - commodities:

Machinery, motor vehicles, pharmaceuticals and other chemicals, fuels, aircraft, plastics, iron and steel, wood pulp and paper products, alcoholic beverages, furniture

Imports:

$2.397 trillion (2011 est.)

Country comparison to the world: 1

$2.028 trillion (2010 est.)

Note: external imports, excluding intra-EU trade

Imports - commodities:

Fuels and crude oil, machinery, vehicles, pharmaceuticals and other chemicals, precious gemstones, textiles, aircraft, plastics, metals, ships

Reserves of foreign exchange and gold:

$812.1 billion (31 December 2011)

Note: this includes reserves held by the European Central Bank and euro-zone national central banks; it excludes reserves for non-euro-area members of the EU

Debt - external:

$16.08 trillion (30 June 2011)

Country comparison to the world: 1

$13.72 trillion (30 June 2010)

Exchange rates:

Euros per US dollar -

0.7838 (2012 est.)

0.7185 (2011 est.)

0.755 (2010 est.)

0.7198 (2009 est.)

0.6827 (2008 est.)

Chapter 6: Energy

Electricity - production:

> 3.255 trillion kWh (2011 est.)

> Country comparison to the world: 4

Electricity - consumption:

> 3.037 trillion kWh (2009 est.)

> Country comparison to the world: 4

Crude oil - proved reserves:

> 5.337 billion bbl (1 January 2012 est.)

> Country comparison to the world: 23

Refined petroleum products - production:

> 12.19 million bbl/day (2011 est.)

> Country comparison to the world: 3

Refined petroleum products - consumption:

> 13.3 million bbl/day (2011 est.)

> Country comparison to the world: 3

Refined petroleum products - exports:

> 2.196 million bbl/day (2009 est.)

> Country comparison to the world: 2

Refined petroleum products - imports:

> 8.613 million bbl/day (2009 est.)

> Country comparison to the world: 2

Natural gas - production:

> 167.6 billion cu m (2011 est.)

> Country comparison to the world: 4

Natural gas - consumption:

461.5 billion cu m (2011 est.)

Country comparison to the world: 4

Natural gas - exports:

93.75 billion cu m (2010 est.)

Country comparison to the world: 5

Natural gas - imports:

420.6 billion cu m (2010 est.)

Country comparison to the world: 2

Natural gas - proved reserves:

2.005 trillion cu m (1 January 2012 est.)

Country comparison to the world: 19

Chapter 7: Communications

Telephones - main lines in use:

     226 million (2011)

Telephones - mobile cellular:

     629 million (2011)

Internet country code:

     .eu; note - see country entries of member states for

     individual country codes

Internet hosts:

     201,116; note - this sum reflects the number of Internet

     hosts assigned the .eu Internet country code (2012)

Internet users:

     247 million (2006)

Chapter 8: Transportation

Airports:

>3,294 (2012)

Airports - with paved runways:

>Total: 1,933

>Over 3,047 m: 117

>2,438 to 3,047 m: 332

>1,524 to 2,437 m: 513

>914 to 1,523 m: 417

>Under 914 m: 554 (2012)

Airports - with unpaved runways:

>Total: 1,361

>Over 3,047 m: 1

>1,524 to 2,437 m: 14

>914 to 1,523 m: 249

>Under 914 m: 1,097 (2012)

Heliports:

>91 (2012)

Railways:

>Total: 228,710 km (2010)

Roadways:

>Total: 5,814,080 km (2010)

Waterways:

>44,103 km (2010)

Ports and terminals:

Antwerp (Belgium), Barcelona (Spain), Braila (Romania), Bremen (Germany), Burgas (Bulgaria), Constanta (Romania), Copenhagen (Denmark), Galati (Romania), Gdansk (Poland), Hamburg (Germany), Helsinki (Finland), Las Palmas (Canary Islands, Spain), Le Havre (France), Lisbon (Portugal), London (UK), Marseille (France), Naples (Italy), Peiraiefs or Piraeus (Greece), Riga (Latvia), Rotterdam (Netherlands), Stockholm (Sweden), Talinn (Estonia), Tulcea (Romania), Varna (Bulgaria)

Chapter 9: Military

Military - note:

The five-nation Eurocorps - created in 1992 by France, Germany, Belgium, Spain, and Luxembourg - has deployed troops and police on peacekeeping missions to Bosnia-Herzegovina, Macedonia, and the Democratic Republic of the Congo and assumed command of the ISAF in Afghanistan in August 2004; Eurocorps directly commands the 5,000-man Franco-German Brigade, the Multinational Command Support Brigade, and EUFOR in Bosnia and Herzegovina; in November 2004, the EU Council of Ministers formally committed to creating 13 1,500-man battle groups by the end of 2007, to respond to international crises on a rotating basis; 22 of the EU's 27 nations have agreed to supply troops; France, Italy, and the UK formed the first of three battle groups in 2005; Norway, Sweden, Estonia, and Finland established the Nordic Battle Group effective 1 January 2008; nine other groups are to be formed; a rapid-reaction naval EU Maritime Task Group was stood up in March 2007 (2007)

Chapter 10: Transnational Issues

Disputes - international:

As a political union, the EU has no border disputes with neighboring countries, but Estonia has no land boundary agreements with Russia, Slovenia disputes its land and maritime boundaries with Croatia, and Spain has territorial and maritime disputes with Morocco and with the UK over Gibraltar; the EU has set up a Schengen area - consisting of 22 EU member states that have signed the convention implementing the Schengen agreements or "acquis" (1985 and 1990) on the free movement of persons and the harmonization of border controls in Europe; these agreements became incorporated into EU law with the implementation of the 1997 Treaty of Amsterdam on 1 May 1999; in addition, non-EU states Iceland and Norway (as part of the Nordic Union) have been included in the Schengen area since 1996 (full members in 2001), Switzerland since 2008, and Liechtenstein since 2011 bringing the total current membership to 26; the UK (since 2000) and Ireland (since 2002) take part in only some aspects of the Schengen area, especially with respect to police and criminal matters; nine of the 12 new member states that joined the EU since 2004 joined Schengen on 21 December 2007; of the three remaining EU states,

Romania and Bulgaria may join by late 2012, while Cyprus' entry is held up by the ongoing Cyprus dispute

Other Key Facts™ Titles

Key Facts on Syria

Key Facts on China

Key Facts on Qatar

Key Facts on India

Key Facts on Germany

Key Facts on Argentina

Key Facts on Russia

Key Facts on North Korea

Key Facts on Brazil

Key Facts on Italy

Key Facts on the United Arab Emirates

Key Facts on the European Union

Key Facts on Pakistan

Key Facts on Saudi Arabia

Key Facts on Cyprus

Key Facts on Iran

Key Facts on Afghanistan

THE INTERNATIONALIST®

2013

www.internationalist.com